# Unexpected Results

## Exploring the Edges of Consciousness

## Marilyn Beech

"....I seem to see mankind as gradually
appropriating to itself the necessary information
through mere attention, *not reason....*"
- *Lawrence Durrell, Balthazar*

Unexpected Results
Exploring the Edges of Consciousness

©2015 Marilyn Beech

ISBN-13: 978-1517144449
ISBN-10: 1517144442

Printed in the United States of America

# Contents:

# 1: Setting the Stage

This is a handbook for people who need to change, but need to stop trying to fix and change themselves. Transformational change is a creative process that is easily derailed by our great ideas about how we work. I have spent 23 years as a Rofling® Structural Integrator and it is through this work that I have come to realize that sometimes people try too hard, think too much, know too little, and as a consequence, get in their own way. They need to learn to follow their bodies instead of lead them. This handbook is a verbal guide in getting yourself started in the process of "Standing Around" – or, how to get out of the way of your body as it leads you towards the next best place. Which is usually, an unexpected place.

We live in the Age of Words. We think *about* life more often than we experience and feel ourselves alive. It seems obvious that we should identify with our thoughts, and that our conscious selves are the thinkers of these thoughts.

It is the thesis of this small book that there is a lot of knowledge (and many functional processes that rely on that knowledge) that have always been part of all life and that continue to function in a big way in the human animal. Our attention has become focused on thought and pretty much stays there, so we do not notice these still-functioning pathways.

But what if, in the long development of conscious thinking, we have merely let these other forms of knowledge atrophy? And what if those other forms actually enhanced many of the functions that we've categorized and named as physical, mental, and emotional? What if knowledge pathways that never lead to word formation or rational thought were actually more effective at directing our lives in some circumstances?

Like a muscle that has atrophied from disuse and then exercised back to full function, it has been my experience that nonverbal knowledge pathways are only in a state of atrophy and can also be "exercised" back into full use. Although, I'm not sure if it is actually the pathway that has atrophied or if it is the attention to that pathway that needs rebuilding. There is something about attention that enlivens and strengthens whatever it is attending to.

Our nervous systems are highly complex with a myriad of functions, one of them the ability to create language. Language is learned – we do not come programmed to speak words. And because of this our ability to talk about what we feel is proscribed by the vocabulary we have managed to put together. This may actually limit or change what we can attend to. What I would like to do with this manuscript is help you become able to return to a state of existence that lets you become aware of non-verbal, or pre-verbal, input (and perhaps output) from your total system. We will use the neural functions of attention and awareness to accomplish this, and we will unlearn the habit of directed, intentional problem-solving. And mostly, we will learn to pause. My hope is that you will be able to exercise your awareness and attention back to robust use, and let the habits of intentionality and directedness atrophy enough that they lose their "habit" status and become a conscious choice once more.

Before we begin I would like us to be clear on what I mean by attention and awareness. They are not the same thing in this way of working with them. Awareness precedes attention, but only by a hair, at least at the start of the "de-atrophying" process.

Awareness happens when your system picks up information. Attention happens when you consciously notice that your system has picked up information. ("Information" does not just come as thoughts and words – with all of our verbally based technology these days that might not be obvious.)

Information is sometimes encoded as words, but more often it comes as sensation. This form of information is not something current culture teaches us to pay attention to unless it has reached the point of pain or pleasure. After doing this work for awhile I've come to realize that there are other information pathways besides the verbal and sensual as well, but we have no useful words for them that would illuminate what I mean so I'll leave them unnamed.

When awareness reaches the "attention" phase, it becomes possible to put words to that sensation (or thought). They might not be entirely accurate, but we can at least make an attempt to verbally approximate whatever showed up. Awareness is often non-verbal. It is the recognition of something going on in your system – but the "recognizer" may easily be a neuron in the motor cortex automatically assessing where down is right now. When we do notice an awareness we tend to instantly put a word, a meaning, and sometimes a whole history to the sensation. Here is where our conscious attention can intervene on itself and begin to loosen the habit of the quick word search and give our systems more pre-verbal time. It is in this consciously attended pre-verbal pause-before-word where we find the unexpected result waiting to present itself.

One of those functions that I and others have experienced is how this self-referencing attention can spur the self-repair of some kinds of system-wide malfunctions. Note that I'm not claiming medical healing, nor would I ever recommend substituting this work for medical intervention. But in general, I feel that our culture's approach to medical "problems" is too narrow. There is much more connectedness and relatedness amongst our body systems than we can imagine and the habit of working with symptoms and parts bypasses the convoluted processes of a world spun of relationships. As we pay more attention to these patterns, relationships, and processes, medical interventions will change, but that is a ways down the road.

My experiences with this work have also led me to feel that another function we will come to know better might be called "connectedness". The strong connections within our systems will become obvious quickly as you do this work, but it seems like connections with other people, animals, plants, cars, buildings, systems, processes, and everything else, exist; and this kind of non-intentional attention either makes those connections stronger or else makes them more noticeable. You may experience this sooner or later, and if you do, just notice what happens. Perhaps someday we'll have enough information to know what's going on.

Above all, the process I will describe shortly is one of absolute experience – no interpretation, no logic, no reason, no judgment, no evaluation allowed! Just pure experience.

There is a part of our brain that is constantly in search of meaning, and will often create rationales that have little to do with reality sometimes, just to satisfy its need for meaning. This work gives us a period of time to let that function stop overworking. It provides a momentary pause between awareness and action, between the experience and the interpretation. It's a way to "fuddle up" the automatic queuing of a reaction that follows some event that our systems have delegated a particular meaning to. This consciously driven pause is not what our systems expect so they stall out momentarily and are forced to take in more information than they usually do. More information about what is going on right this minute (instead of whatever minute in the past the habitual behavior was learned), and to perhaps toss out to our conscious brain a few more tidbits about something going on internally or externally. It provides a momentary arena in which the information that is locked in our non-verbal functions can surface consciously. It will not come as words, but it does come as knowledge, as information that all parts of our systems can use to reconfigure all pertinent relationships. Once you've had an experience of that kind of knowledge surfacing from the depths you will know what I mean.

Observational work is not new – people from J. Krishnamurti to Edgar Tolle have experienced and written about it. The first person, to my knowledge, to bring the entire body, blood, muscle, lungs, personality, everything, into the observational arena was Dr. Marvin Solit. He began his professional career as an Osteopathic physician and early Certified Rolfer™. He came to realize that the therapeutic intervention itself made it impossible for certain kinds of healing to happen. He began playing with self-observation of physical sensation and taking the brakes off the body's un-programmed natural actions. He discovered that this led slowly towards an unwinding of painful patterns, both physical and behavioral.

Coming from a medical profession, Dr. Solit, along with a growing community, were interested in health and pain relief. The idea of repairing and healing the entire human system by a process of unwinding that occurs spontaneously under self-observation is where they initially headed (and found results!). Later some of us found that this was also a process in which information, previously unknown, would sometimes arise. Once in awhile I became aware that I could sense a programmed habit in the split second before it fired off, and that was when I realized that with non-directed observation we have a very powerful new tool. To be able to "see" the brain suddenly initiate some action or thought is to be able to intervene in its learned programming before the action or thought has come into existence. We *can* lose the automatic man! It's rather exciting actually.

People who have engaged in the kind of meditation that is not directed in any way instead of the more directed versions like visualizations, watching the breath, or chanting, will have become familiar with how to use consciousness in this way. There are four modifications still to make to this kind of "meditation": first, that you begin with standing and avoid sitting entirely; second, that you begin your focusing on whatever comes to your attention first, no matter what it is; third, that you set aside all background theory, dogma, or meaning; and fourth, do not call this meditation. Words are laden with meaning and interpretation – that's their function. Dr. Solit called this work "Non-Directed Body Movement". He was never happy with the name and I have found it cumbersome and too full of meaning as well. As this is a process for getting underneath our habitual interpretations, let's begin with as clean a slate as possible.

In keeping with the understanding that this work is about pure experience, I will first give you the rules of the road – the "how to" of what some of us have come to call "standing around". We have to call it something so we can talk to each other, and this is the most interpretively neutral thing I could come up with. Feel free to call it whatever you like. I would suggest that once you've read the how-to section, put the book down and start "standing around". But, no rules, no expectations – follow your own nose on this and see what happens. Remember, whatever results may or may not arise will be unexpected.....and then something else will happen.

# 2: The How-To of "Standing Around"

This work is entirely experiential. It is likely that there are explanations for these experiences in the scientific literature, but that is not important or necessary for this work to be effective. This work is about training our consciously held awareness to take its place as a *part* of our whole system instead of experiencing it in our usual manner as something that stands outside looking in with goals, plans, judgments and meanings. This section is all you really need – the rest of the book is what has come from my experience with this work. You will most likely be able to write an entirely different one. So without a long preamble I will start you out with the basic instructions:

**1.** Start standing, with eyes closed. You won't necessarily remain standing. Lying down seems to work well also. Sitting is problematic - it is usually a position that controls body movements, restricting the ability of tissues to spontaneously move which they will need to do eventually. Many of our habits are programmed into the motor cortex and if any of that material is going to get challenged then the entire body will need to be able to adjust itself. Notice whatever comes to your awareness *first*. This may be a physical sensation, an emotion, or a stream of thoughts.

**2.** If it is a physical sensation that comes to your awareness first, then continue to attend to what it feels like, not *how* it feels, but *what* you feel. We will call this *felt-sense* for the rest of this manuscript. Notice things like where it is in your body, if it moves, intensifies, disappears, what sort of sensation it is – buzzy, tingly, hot, sharp, bubbly, etc. Scan the rest of your body and see if anything comes to your awareness. Please keep noticing how often you return to thinking about the sensation, and how it feels to you instead of what it feels like.  This gets you directly into a judgment about it, a thought-pattern that you don't need to try to get rid of necessarily, but you do need to become aware of your judgments and how much you'd like to act on them. (But don't!)

**3.** If it is an emotion that comes to your attention first, notice the word you've used to describe it – sad, angry, depressed, peaceful, loving, etc. Then remove the word you've used to describe it: de-label it. Just pretend like it has no word to reference it by and turn your attention to *what* you feel – again, not *how* you feel (we have a lot of prejudice about emotions – some are 'good', some 'bad'). Every emotion does indeed have physical sensations (which may actually arise first). Once you've found the felt sense, track it as in #2.

A note about emotions: they come and go as you unwind your past habits. Some people are afraid of unwinding because they do not want to be overwhelmed by uncontrollable emotions. It has been my experience that you never get overwhelmed if you de-label the emotion and attend to the felt-sense. The whole pattern can then truly unwind. This is very different than the practice of "getting it all out" or "releasing emotions" in which emotions tend to escalate and become overwhelming and dramatic - this seems to only practice the emotion, not unwind it.

**4.** If it is a stream of thoughts that come to your awareness first, notice what sort of thoughts they are. Don't stop the thinking; rather, develop an attention to the thinking. This is easier to do if you attend not so much to the content of the thought, but to a larger category: for instance, if you find yourself dwelling on how your spouse ticked you off last night by not coming home in time to get to the movie and you didn't know where s/he was... instead of attending to the details of the event, notice that your thoughts are caught in a past event that could be categorized as a timing problem, or a broken promise, or uncertainty. Some larger category that would encompass thoughts about this event and others that you've experienced previously. Then see if it is possible to detect any physical sensation or posture that arises with the stream of thoughts. If you can detect any, then attend to the felt sense as in #2. If you cannot detect any felt-sense then continue to be aware of your thoughts – categorizing them instead of getting caught up in the story they are trying to draw your attention to. Keep checking for felt-sense – it'll show up sooner or later.

Sometimes people cannot detect anything physical at all. This seems to happen especially often when there has been a physical trauma and the defense at the time was to disappear into a cerebral state and separate completely from what was happening. This is the "out of body" experience. If this is the case, just keep paying attention to the stream of thoughts. Sooner or later that distracting thought pattern has been noticed so often it will begin to falter. You will probably notice the falter by an odd emotion such as frustration, fear, or a sudden vacancy accompanied by not knowing what to do next. This is progress. If an emotion arises in place of the thought, attend to the emotion, de-label it and see if it's possible to detect any physical sensation.

**5.** Once you are able to attend and track the felt-sense you will begin the process of learning to follow instead of lead. When your tissues begin to unwind they do it physically - your body will begin to move of its own accord, with no direction or decision-making on your part. Usually the movements begin slowly as if "they had a mind of their own" (which they do in a way). If you are uncertain whether a movement is a true unwinding or whether you actually decided to do it, put yourself back into your original position and see if the movement happens again, paying attention to your thoughts to notice any orders you may be giving yourself.

If the movement happens again then it's a true non-directed movement motivated by the reassessment going on in your tissues. Allow this to happen, continuing to keep your attention on it. This is the process of following. We are so used to leading – by directing our bodies and our lives – that learning to follow our tissues will be a bit difficult. A new experience anyway!

That's it basically. This is a good place to start. Just stand up, close your eyes, and see what comes to your attention first. The following are tips about situations that commonly arise for people but may not for you.

**6. A Word about Intention:**
We rarely make a move without a goal in mind. Being goal-oriented is part of our culture, education and sense of well-being. There are many situations where directedness is very helpful and necessary. But if we wish to loosen up our attachment to past events and conditioned habits, then we need to learn to follow the movements of our tissues instead of leading them. To do this we need to have no intention whatsoever. We must approach our system with attention, but with no intention to accomplish anything. No desire to make something feel better, discover something more about ourselves, unwind a particular incident, get rid of a nagging pain. There is only what is happening exactly NOW.

Intention is often driven unconsciously by previous experience. Once you've had an experience of something changing while you're unwinding, you're going to expect that, or something like it, to happen again. It's pretty much impossible for that expectaton not to arise. It's frustrating, but you'll get so you can see those expectations and then all you have to do is observe them. Don't try to make them go away, they won't. Just observe them because they've now become part of who you are. In my experience with this work, the more I've observed expectation in my system the less hold I feel that it has over my next thoughts, actions, movements, etc. It becomes a fairly thin veneer that gets out of the way quickly once it's observed again.

## 7. A Second Word about Intention: The Pause.
Once we manage to begin standing around without a goal in mind the next place many of us get sidetracked is the nearly automatic response of trying to "make something feel better". The big Fix. It's an automatic habit in Western culture (and maybe in others). Once we've discovered a symptom that's uncomfortable we search for some way to make it "go back the way it was before". Notice yourself doing this. You may not be able to catch yourself at it right away. Well-learned habits are hard to even notice.

Once you've noticed an attempt to fix things don't give yourself a hard time about it. Instead, just give yourself a pause before you act on your inclination. The pause is very important. Attend to what you are feeling – physically – and track whatever happens next. The "fix-it action" is sometimes a way to distract yourself from damage that was done earlier and your system thinks you need to ignore it. It can be a defense to keep you out of unsafe territory. Or it may be the technique you've learned to get yourself through life with this damage intact. And much of the time it is just pain dug-in neural habit.

When we have had an injury, whether physical, emotional or both, our systems go to great lengths to keep us safe. We will unconsciously put together an endless variety of physical, emotional or mental distractions to keep us from paying attention to old damage. This is not a bad thing - our systems are trying to keep us alive at all costs and these distracting elements are a good way to do it. Our systems just haven't caught up with what's happening now

- that we are no longer in danger. So, give yourself a pause before taking action. Notice what you feel, (not how you feel), and return to following the movements and feelings in your tissues instead of leading them.

It's really just a matter of updating the software that got programmed for some other time and experience. Our systems understand the varied pressures of experience, not the weight of words, so they need to experience their old programming in a fully aware present-time habitat where nothing life-threatening is going on and you are entirely safe. By observing your system through its felt-sense in present time, the outdated programming will automatically update, and your non-conscious attachments to physical, emotional and behavioral patterns that are the result of old trauma and injury thin out. They become something akin to a ghost of itself that you can feel wander lightly through your system on occasion, but they no longer run you.

**8. Another Reason to Pause:**
Allowing yourself to pause before taking action breaks into an existing habit pattern. In so doing, more information is allowed to surface. Perhaps it isn't verbally accessible knowledge, at least not yet, but it will be understandable to the rest of your non-verbal system. Information about the damage you've incurred that's been suppressed, ignored, or bulldozed over with medications, training, education, exercises, surgeries, or fix-it techniques, will begin to make an appearance.

This is very interesting stuff, and it's all your very own individual history that no one in the world could tell you about. But please, don't *expect* it to show up…or at least watch your expectations as they arise.

**9. A Word about Resistance:**
Resistance is something we do in the service of Intention. If we have a goal then we fight off challenges to that goal. We can get into subtle resistance patterns with this unwinding work. Since the unwinding occurs at the tissue level we often try to keep our attention on our felt-sense when, for example, it may be our thoughts that are really active. Many people have trained in meditation techniques where you control thinking by letting the thoughts go and returning your attention to breathing. With this

work, that would be a resistance technique - taking your attention off what's happening and placing it elsewhere. If you notice that all you can do is go cerebral, then go cerebral - just notice it, notice it with complete attention. You want to step outside your thoughts, not "be" your thoughts, watch them.

Another common resistance is to stretch in response to a contracting pattern. The inclination to stretch when something feels tight is pretty automatic as well as highly approved of in many circles. But in this work it is generally a "distracting behavior" – something to keep you away from letting the contraction embedded in your system finish itself. Instead, just pause, notice the desire to stretch, and return your attention to what is contracting. Attend to the state of your system exactly as it is right now. When you can do that it will then take you to the next best place it can go.

## 10. The Next Best Place:
This process is not linear. We're used to getting a bit better each day – a slow progression from where we are to someplace else. For one thing, "better" has no meaning in this work. What we are doing is unfettering our systems from a lifetime of habits - motor habits, thought habits, behavior habits, or habitual patterns in connective tissues that hold us in place. Some were intentionally learned, some are responses to danger or injury, and some just come about because we are a plastic object in a strong gravity field. Most are the result of an entirely normal brain function. What you will be when freer of all that is unknown as yet. It may be "better" or it may be something else entirely. The body persists in repairing itself; programmed habits of any sort can get in the way of that repair. All we are doing is putting some space between a perceived need to do something and the doing of it.

When we back off from leading our systems and learn to follow, then our bodies will unwind whatever is most available. Whatever is next on *its* agenda. We have no idea what that might be, but in retrospect I understand that the process takes the path of least resistance, often leaving you in a new place (physically or emotionally) for awhile before unwinding further. There seems to be no optimal, perfect place to get to. Or if there is, it seems to be a state of complete adaptability – being able to change as the situation necessitates. But I don't know anyone who's actually gotten there, so I'm just guessing about that.

This is also not to be misconstrued as "going with the flow", which is often used as an excuse to just be passive or lazy. It's really a way to be non-participatory. This observational awareness is very active, very participatory. And total awareness of what-is (the "flow") is not the same as going with it...it is noticing it, not actively going anywhere, and waiting for the body system to take itself where it needs to go next. There will be times of non-action and times of action. As you practice this kind on non-intentional awareness your life will come to be lived in this way – at least a little bit. These action/non-action times will become apparent over time. One thing you'll begin to do is not waste energy taking action when it's actually time to wait awhile.

**11. Intra- and Interpersonal Unwinding:**
Life patterns accumulate in the context of interpersonal relationships; they tend to surface more naturally, therefore, with one or more people present. It is helpful to find another person or even a group to "stand around" with. In the presence of other people habitual tendencies arise that will not arise when you are alone. This gives you the opportunity to let habits and emotional traumas surface and begin the process of relieving yourself of them (not re-living).

But, if no one else is around, then "stand around" by yourself. As you become more attentive to your whole system, not just the verbally conscious part, and learn to follow as often as you lead, then your whole life starts to become an unwinding process. You might notice your system responding uncomfortably when someone calls, or greets you on the street, or someone walks by that has a certain feel to them – when this happens take a mental pause and notice your reactions, the felt-sense of it, and keep doing whatever you're doing, but with this awareness included. In this way you are always doing group work and always individual work.

**12. Pain**
Sometimes movements change into something else: they can repeat themselves endlessly, stop completely, turn into a different movement or an emotional response. Sometimes they cause an intense contraction that can be painful and keep getting more

intense. If this happens don't worry, don't try to stop it, or stretch it, or otherwise fix the situation. You may have discovered an "unfinished action": your body was trying to seize up completely at one time (or many times, like daily at the computer), but you've stopped it before it could finish the movement. This is a common phenomenon with life-threatening trauma like a car accident, attack, long-term emotional abuse, or a surgery. The body is still trying to finish the seizing-up. Let it finish. The contraction will dissipate of its own accord once it's finished the interrupted action.

These contractions can also be the result of unfinished traumas that are still active in the amygdala (the part of the brain responsible for fight, flight and freeze). There is no need to know what caused the contraction – old traumas do not have to be lived through again, contrary to some ways of thinking. Once the tissues have unwound out of the habits they created for themselves the whole thing will become only a boring memory, if even that. Old traumas cannot unwind unless the affects are experienced fully in present-time. It's like updating software. The early version was created at a time of great fear. Now it needs to see itself still operating with that fear-response on high in current-time, when there is nothing horrible going on at all. Once these automatic responses register the banality of the moment as a real-time experience (not a thought, desire or command), and that there is no threat at this time, then they will begin to update their stored content and loosen up from constant over-reaction. It just takes an acute awareness of both the present in all its non-threatening glory and the habitual fear-response as it causes physical, emotional and mental affects.

People learn techniques to interrupt pain because we have judged pain to be a bad thing, and that interrupting pain is a good thing. So we tend to interrupt and try to 'fix' painful situations. Watch for these interrupting habits. Pain isn't necessarily a bad thing; it's focused feelings. The word 'pain', however, adds a frightening judgment to the feelings, making them more difficult to access directly. Learning to fully experience feelings without giving them a name tends to keep us from escalating sensations to the level of drama and leads us to deeper levels of unwinding. When pain arises, do not focus on the label: "pain". Instead, keep your attention on the felt-sense and see what it really feels like.

OK – enough reading. If you haven't already, stand up, shut your eyes, and ask yourself, "what comes to my awareness first?" Then see what happens next.

# 3: Attention-without-Intention

I have found a variety of uses for this kind of awareness work and you will most likely discover others. So far it has been transformational in regard to:
1. making a change in habitual behaviors, thoughts, emotions and in physical structure and movement habits;
2. discovering the true meaning behind a thought or movement pattern;
3. exploring the edges and possibilities of consciousness;
4. unwinding physical and behavioral patterns – getting the flow going again;
5. unexpected resolutions to just about anything.

## *The feedback loop*
There is the science of consciousness and then there is the experience of consciousness. The science has been getting very interesting in the last couple of decades, and one of the current writers on this subject (David Eagleman, *Incognito*, Pantheon Books a division of Random House, NY, 2011) describes the role of consciousness as the controlling function, the "decider" for those many instances when the conflicting functions of the brain need to choose between options. Consciousness is the future planner, the goal-setter, the decision-maker that keeps the whole shebang pointed in a specific direction. We'll call this one the "Overseer".

It is the thesis of this manuscript that this is not the only function of consciousness. This goal-planner aspect of consciousness can be understood as the overseer of the logical, rational aspects of our brains. The one that chooses between options that are presented to it. But there is an equally important "master observer" in charge of a very different function: that of the non-directed, participatory, system-wide, non-linear, experiential, immediate awareness of exactly what-is-happening-now processes. This function of consciousness is better described as the necessary link that closes the feedback loop of self-referencing. We'll call this function the "Observer".

One of the attributes of pure observation is that it has no directedness to it – no intention aside from the intention to observe. All other action, expectation, or desire for consequences, is not involved. This is not something we are commonly taught – will-powering our way through the world is more normal. But it is evolution's recent gift of a self-referencing consciousness that does make it possible for us to engage in pure observation.

Many of our physical functions use self-referencing feedback loops – all of our hormones work in this manner. For example, thyroid hormone levels in the bloodstream are monitored by chemical sensors in a part of the brain called the hypothalamus. When levels fall unacceptably low the hypothalamus secretes thyrotropin-releasing hormone (TRH). This hormone releases a chemical message to another part of the brain to start secreting thyroid-stimulating hormone (TSH). Finally, this TSH tells the thyroid gland to start producing the thyroid hormones, $T_3$ and $T_4$, which continues until blood levels of thyroid hormones return to homeostatic normal. The hypothalamus picks up this change in blood hormone levels via the chemical sensor/messenger feedback loop and will initiate a reduction in TSH when blood levels get too high. This is just one example of a feedback loop, there are many more.

There is no difference in kind between the feedback loop of the thyroid gland and the feedback loop of consciousness – only a difference in degree and complexity. Conscious attention, observation, can bring all of these multiple feedback loops, the whole neural network, sensory input, conscious and unconscious responses and directives, into one gigantic system of self-referencing feedback. If the Overseer does not step in to direct actions then things begin to change in non-linear, non-rational, non-technical ways. Interesting information shows up as well as behaviors, emotions, thoughts and actions that are not part of one's usual repertoire. This is about throwing a spanner into a system that has built a vocabulary of responsive actions out of genetic, instinctual and learned information. The spanner is your acute attention being focused on a system crying out for something different while not allowing it to continue in its habitual response. What you get are unexpected results.

What kind of results? That's a mystery. These results emerge out of a soup of patterns too numerous to count as the entire system begins to experiment with different ways to act together. It's about relatedness – how all these patterns relate to each other and to the world outside. People have had the experience of chronic structure problems reorganizing themselves to a more comfortable and efficient relationship; old behaviors gradually release their hold and leave the system; recurrent anxiety, depression, PTSD and anger have transformed (to what? many different things); an ability to notice develops with unknown and potentially interesting consequences; addictions lose their stranglehold.

Sometimes new information suddenly shows up, either about the person or about some other subject entirely. An early practitioner of this work felt his way into an entirely new theory of the geometry of electromagnetism that explains the transformation of energy to matter and back again in a very simple and beautiful manner. None of these results came about because anyone was trying to make something in particular happen. This is probably the hardest piece of this work: watching expectations arise and not acting on the expectation; watching desires and "should be's" arise and letting them just be part of the observed. This is important to remember while doing this work.

I have heard it proposed that the only free will we actually have is the ability to veto an action - we do not actually come up with actions "ourselves", merely follow the orders of a complex underground neural machine. That may or may not turn out to be true, but even if it is, even if all our conscious mind gets to do is vote yes or no, the "no vote" is huge. In this work, the combination of noticing what comes up along with not acting on any suggestions that come from the system is what seems to cause the feedback loop to activate. When we do the opposite - allow our systems to go ahead and act on the suggestions it is throwing into awareness, whether they are a thought that we go ahead and "think" because it's our thought after all, or a directive to scratch an itch, or run to the kitchen for cheese - then we do not close the feedback loop and habitual actions, behaviors, emotions, will just continue to arise. The automaton runs on and on.

To engage in this kind of consciously activated feedback loop requires an interesting exploration into our expectations. Every time we learn something (no matter how that gets learned – traumatic car wreck, slowly putting the logic of math into memory, being raised as a male or female in a particular culture), we create an expectation. Once you've spent time being fully aware of a sensation in your knee and had the experience of the sensation disappearing and your knee fully functioning again, then your central nervous system has just set an expectation that the same thing will happen again next time you focus attention. Repair will happen! And you can be sure that it won't. It's that expectation itself that is now in the way.

It is this very exploration of expectation that can help us to get an inkling of the complex machinations of our brains that never come to cognitive consciousness. It will help prevent us from following an already-projected plan of action when it is no longer useful, or find the next best route when you have no idea what that might be. Our consciousness is a huge new toy in nature's evolutionary bag of tricks. As usual with evolution, there was no designer behind the curtain trying to come up with a better mousetrap. New opportunities for adaptation just arise. Conscious awareness is a new opportunity and we get to take it in hand and push it in whatever directions it can go. As a spanner in the works of habitual neural action, I think this new toy we've been given has great entertainment value to say the least. It definitely has evolutionary value – it's up to us to give this function some legs.

Most of the workings of our bodies are non-verbal, and hence, non-conscious. They are *not*, however, non-connected. Our entire systems are constantly in communication via the nervous system, hormonal system, connective tissue system, and others we know nothing about yet. Most of this communication happens below the level of verbal consciousness - or perhaps it's more accurate to say that it happens *before* verbal consciousness. We never consciously know enough to make accurate decisions about what our bodies need to do next on their paths to functional repair. Exercise routines and diets are common ways we do this, and with the best of intentions! Many times these well-intentioned efforts to fix ourselves only makes things worse – again, because we don't consciously know enough to take into account how everything is connected and how everything needs to change to accommodate and support a new normal.

This doesn't mean that we can't find out, however! The way to do that is through non-intentional attention. Our attention is like a flashlight. We can shine it into a dark room, knowing that there is a bookcase there, and point that light in the general direction we think it ought to be. Eventually we'll find that bookcase, but in the meantime the flashlight might have picked up a lot of other things lurking in the dark which do not snag our notice because we are not looking for them. This is intentional attention. It is selective, directed, and not useful for noticing *everything* that's there, only for finding what we've already decided we want to find.

This is the problem with therapies in general. All therapies have a theoretical basis that its practitioners learn. It's a lens therapists have learned to look through and helps them narrow down the possibilities of how to work with this particular person. Some of these lenses are very technical, some are less so. The only person who can ever really understand your body from the inside out is you – and you can only know most of it non-verbally!

Nevertheless, the feedback loop is a process that our bodies have made wide use of and with great success. We can use the feedback loop consciously to aid us as we flash the light around in the dark seeking restoration of function. The key is "non-intentional". We have to put ourselves into an observational mode that lets our flashlights pick up everything without "prejudice", to use a legal term.

### What do you feel?
The observational mode that seems to work the best is to place attention on what is currently being called "felt-sense". This is to distinguish it from 'feelings' which is often used synonymously with 'emotions'. Felt-sense is the awareness of physical sensations of any sort. The most important aspect of this kind of attention is to notice *what* you feel, not *how* you feel. Most of us are not very good at this kind of awareness, at least once we're past childhood. Our education trains us to pay close attention to other things. We often only become aware of felt-sense when something feels terrible, and we learn to notice it by quick judgments – whether it feels good or bad. We nail this thinking down daily when we greet each other with "Hi, how are you?" We learn to *think about* our lives, not *feel* them.

We want to be able to feel more than the painful things and this will take some effort. The best way to approach this kind of attention is to let your awareness rest on whatever felt-sense comes to your attention first, and to use an investigative, or explorer mode instead of judgmental. We are usually quite habituated to making quick determinations about what a feeling means, whether it's ok or not, needs to be different, etc. You will do this automatically when you first get started, and mostly likely for a long time to come! Its actually part of our defense system and perhaps embedded in how neurons work. But it can lead us astray and this is where our awareness-used-as-a-feedback-loop can correct habits of meaning that are inaccurate or perhaps too generalized.

But, that's getting ahead of ourselves. As an aid to helping our systems find a new normal, non-intentional attention lets us connect consciously (but not verbally) with everything in our systems. The flashlight gets to pick up everything in the dark room, not just what we are looking for, and not just things we already know about. The body is in communication with itself anyway, but transformative change seems to become more possible when we participate consciously (but without intention). I have noticed this happen over and over during the last 20 years and do not have an explanation for it - I only know that it happens.

It may be that felt-sense information comes to have both conscious and non-conscious meanings associated with it (through a connection between interoceptors and the neocortex). We build these associations through experience and over time the sensation becomes automatically linked to a set meaning. When we pay attention to felt-sense input but do not allow any automatic responses, then we are forcing our systems to look at these associated meanings in what might be a slightly new context. The meanings have to be adjusted and then some other process can come into play. The whole system can readjust itself and find something different to do with an area that's not functioning very well.

You can play with this kind of attention next time you're outside: find a tree and then take the label "tree" away – you no longer have a word for this thing. Now you have to discover what it is. You will most likely start noticing things about this particular tree that you never noticed before, and perhaps you'll even start wondering what life is like from the inside of the tree instead of from the outside looking in. This is where we want to get with our own systems – what are all these various parts doing from *their* perspectives, not the ones we've come to place on them? Their perspectives will not be verbally accessible. But they are felt-sense accessible and perhaps over time you will develop a new vocabulary that accurately describes what you feel of them. (I've been accused often of making up odd but descriptive words.) Sometimes the meaning of a felt-sense will arise in an intuitive or visual way, and will become something you can eventually put a word to. When you enter into a human system with a non-intentional flashlight all kinds of interesting things can show up. What's really interesting is that this is all unique to you – your own past and present that you are the only real authority on, and out of which will flow your future. It will flow differently when you start using the non-intentional feedback loop.

### What comes to your attention first:
This is important – this is one of the things that makes this work very different from most other kinds of attention practices. You are not going to put your attention on something in particular, like breath, or thoughts, or feeling your blood move through arteries. You are not going to try to empty yourself of content. You are going to let your system select the content you will attend to.

Merely shut your eyes and notice whatever snags your attention *first*. This will be the entry (whether it's a thought, an emotion, or a physical feeling) into whatever it is that your system is most in need of addressing. Think of it as the thread you pull in a sweater that can unravel the whole thing, but you have no idea what route it's going to take or what's going to surface as it comes undone. Sometimes it is not clear what to attend to – many things seem to vie for attention all at the same time. Attend to all of them globally – it feels like holding your attention lightly and evenly on everything. Then notice when you start to become snagged by one of them more than the others.

Sometimes nothing at all comes to your attention. In this case, just wait, holding a global attention on your whole system – no focus on anything in particular. Something will eventually crop up. It may be a thought-stream about how boring this all is and maybe nothing will happen at all. Don't dismiss a thought such as this. Put another way, don't take the content of this thought as the important message. The important message is the thought itself, that it is constructed with a content designed to get your decision-making self to stop doing this attention work and get busy with daily life activities. If you follow those instructions you will very effectively keep all your old habits, traumas and injuries right where they are. Nothing will change. If you stay with the thought, however, using it as the thread you are going to attach your awareness to, things may indeed change. Perceive this thought as a portal into your personal unknown, then find whatever physical feelings are present and track them like you would an animal through the brush. Again, we are not attempting to become empty of content, we are noticing and tracking the content that our system (not our "thinker") has decided to present us with.

# 4: Habit

Humans have little or no instinctive behaviors. Our behaviors are mostly learned, which makes us extremely adaptable. But an ability to adapt readily seems to be an illusive trait. People hold onto rigid traditions, ideals, ideologies, theories, perceptions, behaviors, postures, and ways of moving - all conditioned by education of some sort or another, and all on automatic pilot. We are more *Homo automaticus* than *sapiens*. We think that our decision-making function means we are free-will creative thinkers, acting on our best judgments. But in fact, most of our decisions come out of a lifetime of habitual thinking, neural programming, unexamined assumptions, learned socialization, imposed values, and the necessity to find some way to decide what to do about things. Having an opinion means you are mature and able to evaluate a situation. But are we even a little bit close to being able to evaluate a situation clearly?

I don't think we are, not until we've eradicated habit from our systems. As long as we are in the grip of habits we cannot perceive clearly nor are we free. We can fight and yearn for freedom all we want, but until we can choose what we are going to do, say, think, and act on, then we are not really free.

Our habits are rife throughout our whole systems. We have habits of posture that we started as babies – perhaps the result of physical impairments, perhaps just a matter of imitating parents. We have habits of walking, sitting, breathing. We have emotional habits we've developed from our early childhood responses to survival. We have habitual thought patterns that we identify with so completely that we think they are "us".

This kind of non-intentional-attention is an effective way for habits to become known to us, and through the use of the pause, to wedge open a little distance before the habit rolls on down its preferred pathway without a second thought. The pause gives us a chance to have that second thought, and noticing everything that comes to our attention just before that habit gets started is the path of change. Changing to what? Well, most likely not what you expect or have decided that you desire. It'll probably be better than that, but unexpected. And it may take noticing the habit many times.

Much of the stress in our physical systems, which manifests itself as inflammation in various tissues and/or mental issues, is the result of "old motors" that got started sometime in our lives and continue to run. These old motors could also be called adhesions, blockages, traumas, habits, education - whatever put them there is a lengthy list! Much of the energy in our systems is tied up in these old motors. A surgery, no matter how important it was in saving your life, most likely left new motors running which will soon turn to old motors: the trauma (from your body's point of view) of being knocked unconscious and stabbed with a knife, the suffocating sensation of having a breathing tube shoved down your throat, the cutting out of an organ, the pounding in of a new joint spike. These actions saved your life, left their mark, and can lead to further unhappiness. But they can also be unwound.

This kind of exploration requires what I call "the explorer's mind". Pretend you are setting off on an adventure to a place you've never been. You look at everything with keen observation, not knowing what's around the next corner, not knowing who will show up and how you will communicate. You know nothing. And you don't know what will happen next. You only know that you are participating in life right this minute. This is the explorer's mind. Cultivate this and let it become how you approach every second of waking life. It's that simple, and that difficult.

# 5: The Next-Best-Place

One of the very important tenets of this work is that there is no perfect place to reach. The idea of the perfect way to be, the perfect this, or the perfect that, is not conducive to transformational change or repair.

There are two parts to this.

One is that if we are going to strive for perfect, then we actually have to know before getting there what perfect is. Since we have never been to this perfect place, we can only imagine it. And we can only imagine something we don't know about by accessing information about what we *do* know about – our experience or education. The past, in other words. If there is something about our behavior that we do not like, and we are going to come up with the perfect way to be, we pretty much have to just imagine up the opposite of whatever it is we don't like about ourselves. So we've now made up a goal to reach, and put ourselves into conflict with who we are right now. Now there is conflict to deal with as well as whatever the objectionable behavior was. We've escalated the problem. Some Buddhist doctrines tell us that tension and pain are natural and unavoidable responses to imbalance, but suffering is optional. Conflict is suffering. And it is optional.

The second part to this is that when we have a known goal in mind, that goal always limits what our systems can do. Our systems try valiantly to make our desires come about. Often they can't – there are just too many connections that can't get made. But they do try. And in trying to go towards that projected goal, all other opportunities for change are missed, bulldozed over, ignored. And where do we get the idea that we know what's best for ourselves, for our family, for our planet? Well, from a lot of places, but for now, if we could just let in the notion that perhaps we *don't* know best, and never have, and don't have any way of knowing what's best, we might actually make something really different happen. Something that will turn out to be the next best thing.

When we take the conflict between what-we-are-now and what-we-desire out of the picture by getting rid of that projected goal, we open up our systems to deal with whatever is most in its way right this minute. What that is will be defined not just by who you are, but who you are in your environment at this point in time. Our systems are in total connection with themselves. As well, our systems are in total connection with other systems – other people, present or not, other animals, plants, perhaps even with non-living systems like rocks and mountains. Much of this is like an iceberg – under the realm of conscious knowledge. Conscious knowledge is only part of what is known – what our systems know. The rest is "under water", but still connected nonverbally to everything it is possible to be connected with.

When you attend to what you feel, with the explorer's mind and with no projected goal, then you've put yourself into a transformational feedback system. Biology works on a feedback loop – remember how the thyroid hormone feedback loop works.

To enter into this feedback loop with self-reflective attention, whatever comes to our attention first is not acted on, nothing is consciously done about it. Your attention, with no directiveness attached, feeds that awareness back into the whole system. Something happens then that stops automatic action in its tracks, gets the system to wake up again and re-assess what is actually going on right this minute. The habitual action is waylaid and more information can be brought into the system.

The consequence of that is often a change in response. It can then start making adjustments throughout the whole system, so that a bit better total situation can then arise. This is the *next best place*. It's not the perfect place. It is only the next place your whole system-in-its-environment-right-now can get to and have it be the best it can do for everything and everyone involved. Keep in mind that whatever changes are going to occur in you, all of the connections you presently have with everything/everyone else are involved as well. We cannot possibly know what all those connections are. But the nonverbal information embedded in all systems works out the next best transformative change with the most favorable changes for all. Including you.

This is the feedback loop in action. For it to work optimally we cannot be trying to accomplish an action ourselves. That will thwart the whole process. This is how we've gotten into trouble with ourselves and the resources of our planet. Our technological and political changes have been made in a connection vacuum. We've made them based on what we've learned, what we can put into words, and what we can project from that. Most information in our world is not verbal, much more than is verbal. The next best thing arises by literally feeling our way, so that the nonverbal information has a chance to be included in our decision-making.

The next step, once the next best place has been formed, is to *notice* that next best place. Notice it using felt sense, but now we can add words to it – the experience has happened and we can put words around it. This helps us to establish that next best place, to recognize it and to let it expand. This is how we use verbal consciousness well. First by noticing what-is, then noticing the next what-is. Attention, not intention or desire.

It is also a good idea to try not to interpret this experience. This gets us back into abstractions and generalizations, so that the next time we go into feedback-loop-mode we will often assume that something similar will happen. It won't. The same thing never happens twice. This is because we are now different, and everything that we are connected to is now different, and the present time environment is always different. Learning to feel and notice the subtleties of what is different is very important.
We are always moving towards the next best place, and then the next best place after that, and so on. Losing the rigidities, the defenses, the motors that run us is not a linear path of going from here to there. It's more like a zig-zag, or wandering path and you never know how it's going to turn you next. But it is always pointing you towards the next best place, never the next worst. That is something you don't need to have faith in, or believe – that knowledge comes with experience. It is waiting for everyone to come to know.

I have no idea if we ever get to the last of the next best places. I suspect not. Evolution is not something with an endpoint as far as we know and change over time should be able to continue until time comes to an end.

# 6: The Problem of Conflict

When something problematic arises in our lives, whether it's a behavior we're tired of repeating, or pain in the neck after computing all day, or a person at work we get irritated with, or any myriad of things we call problems, we have two routes we can take. One is to figure out what we'd rather have going on and take steps to make that happen. The second is to turn our attention to our own felt-sense and see what happens when we get to know ourselves in this situation fully. The first is a route of conflict – every time we decide that the situation-as-it-is is not good enough and we've got to fix it, then we've put ourselves into conflict with ourselves. This often, very often, leads us into conflict with others.

Now, added to the original problem that has its own energies and discomforts, is this second layer of tension – the conflict we've created between what-is and what-we-want-it-to-be. I would like to suggest (and I'm not the first by any means) that it is the conflict itself that really causes problems for us. Now we have set ourselves up for something we must accomplish, and the failure to accomplish it is something people flagellate themselves with constantly. But even if you are successful in fixing the problem, if you've overcome the pain in the neck by stretching, or stopped yourself from having that next glass of wine with sheer will power, or put that office worker in his place, the original problem has only been controlled. You've gone to war and successfully controlled the problem, which is going to be a problem again in short order. The problem has not disintegrated, nor has anything unknown about why that was a problem in the first place come to the surface.

We do this conflict reaction rather often – you'll probably be quite surprised when you start to notice how many times in a day you make these fix-it decisions and put yourself into conflict. Simply put, the conflict is between what-is and what-should-be. The other route to take is to notice when you've decided on a fix-it plan and are about to put yourself into a conflict. Give yourself a pause and notice everything you possibly can. Notice the thought, the emotions, the physical feelings, the environment outside. Please! Don't try to stop yourself from acting on your fix-it thought – this creates *another* added layer of conflict! Just take the pause and notice everything. This will make it impossible for that unwanted behavior to proceed at this point in time. A new behavior may very well not show up. Or it might. Sometimes the behavior, thought, emotion, etc., just melts away as if it had never existed. Sometimes it doesn't. Results will always be unexpected.

Part of the reason that we end up in conflict is that when problems arise we need to imagine up an alternative. Usually the best alternative we can come up with is the opposite of whatever is going on – if people are yelling at each other then peace is the answer. We do not have enough information or knowledge to know what else to offer up as an alternative – and how often does peace actually erupt just because we want it to? And how often to we keep looking for resolution, peace, etc.? Forcing peace on top of a conflict never works for long. If we need a different result, then we need a different premise and for that we need to let the unknown surface. This can only happen in an environment of awareness and non-directedness.

This is not the same as acceptance. Nor is it non-acceptance. There are many words of wisdom out there exhorting us to accept ourselves for who we are. But this is not what we're up to here. (I haven't found acceptance to be a useful tool for anything actually.) Acceptance is beside the point and has nothing to do with what I'm writing about. It is actually an action we take that puts us in conflict with what we are at this moment in time. It is an abstract way of thinking *about* ourselves which is not conducive to being able to experience.

We cannot experience life if we are thinking that we are now accepting ourselves, with all our "faults." It actually helps us nail in an identity about ourselves "with all our faults", and puts a huge big roadblock in the middle of the path of change. There is absolutely no need to like or accept, or have any judgment at all about whatever state you find yourself in. Pain really does hurt. To accept pain creates an artificial situation and throws you into conflict with what-is (the pain) and what-should-be (accept the pain). To not-accept pain (fight it) is to directly go into conflict with it. Both approaches only produce an un-resolvable conflict that can actually make the pain worse. It can set up a stressful internal milieu that leads to inflammation, which in turn sets up another feedback loop with serious physical consequences. It can certainly create mental suffering.

Conflict merely creates a tension between the state of the human right now, and some created goal of the state the human would rather be in. That tension actually becomes a physical tension, not just a mental one. And extra tension in an already painful body will only amp up the pain. If nothing else, attention on what-is will get rid of this extra layer of tension.

Fear is another emotion that is very common with injury, pain, or interpersonal conflicts. It will also create physical tensions in the body and exacerbate the pain. But again, it's not going to help to try to get rid of the fear, or "release the fear" as some suggest. That's the conflict route again. Instead, notice the fear, what *it* feels like – do the whole attention path on the fear and see what happens with it.


## Creating a goal

One of the reasons that deciding what we would rather be is that we don't have a very good way of figuring that out. Once we realize that some "what-is" about ourselves (behavior, habit, lifestyle, job, hairdo) is problematic, we can only come up with a "better" idea based on what we already know. This knowledge comes from one of two places: we imagine the opposite of whatever the what-is is; or it comes from our education (not just formal schooling but early childhood orientation, culture, the limits of the senses, etc.). There is no room there for the unknown to pop up.

We limit ourselves unconsciously and ignorantly for the most part. Much of the benefit of this kind of attention work is to let the unknown become consciously known. It's actually rather fun. However… if you make that a goal – learning something previously unknown – you'll find yourself in conflict again. This time the conflict is between what you know and the desire to know what you don't know. So always approaching this attention work with attention on what-is, and not on hope or desire is so very important… and difficult. Once you've had the experience doing this work and having unknown information appear, you'll want to have that happen again. Everyone wants that. The only thing you can do is to pay attention to that hope – what it feels like, the thoughts that come up, the expectations and what they feel like. It is always just a matter of turning the attention back on itself. Closing the feedback loop so the information system can adjust itself.

## To goal or not to goal...that *is* the question
Creating a goal is a great way to limit yourself. Now, you may *want* to limit yourself sometimes. In the course of life we do have to get some things done – make a living for instance. Some people really want to experience something in particular and will need all the intention, goal-oriented-ness and perseverance  they can round up.

I am not suggesting that non-intention and not having a goal is the way to live a full life. What I am saying is that you will need to become skilled at knowing which process is appropriate and when. There is a time to push with single-minded purpose, and there is a time to not-know and feel. Ideally, we would have trained one part of the "committee of consciousness" to always stay attendant on what-is, while other parts of the committee get something done. I think this is something we can train ourselves to do but haven't yet.  It's best not to expect too much and then have to go into conflict about being a failure. To do either non-intentional attention work, or to pursue a goal, each at their own time, is sufficient for now. To just be able to discern when you are being goal-oriented, and whether that's even necessary, is a big step. Do that one first.

## Conflict in the larger context
As you come to recognize your habits of creating conflict within yourself, you begin to recognize conflict in other places. You will watch your friends set up conflict between themselves and their partners, or with you. You will see it at school board meetings, city hall, Wall Street, national politics, between countries, ethnic groups, economic groups.

 If you refuse to act on that conflict, but instead be aware of it, you will be able to participate in actually transforming how humans interact as a whole. It's a very important thing to do!

Participation is our responsibility as part of this planetary community. But quality participation is important. Conflictual participation is not helpful. We have too much of that already. To learn to listen completely to what someone in anger or anguish has to say without defense or opposition, just total and complete attention on them and their words is to do something very different in this world. To not react to someone else's conflict, but to see it, hear it, and feel what it does to your system, but not to act on that feeling....that is the very different and potentially transformational action that we can all make in this world. And what is so great about this kind of socially-conscious participation is that it has transformational potential for each of us on a personal level as well. We don't have to be abstractly altruistic! Benefits accrue in our own lives.

# 7: Who's the Authority Here?

An interesting question to ponder as you become more facile with felt-sense awareness and the ability to follow the body's lead is where you find authority. Many people, maybe even most or all, feel more comfortable with some authority outside themselves "laying down the law", as it were.

We seek someone or something larger than us to help us figure out our values, know what is right or wrong behavior, find out what is a good thing to do with our lives. Our favorite targets for this authority are deities, a political agenda, a parent, a spouse, a guru, a philosophy or a science, an author who's written a book that you agree with. You probably have your own favorite authority.

The idea that we might be our own authority can lead to fear, depression, or egocentrism when thought about abstractly or as a goal.  But there is an important difference here –no decision needs to be made about who you will take authority from. It comes about as you unwind bound up patterns in your tissues and limiting patterns in your thoughts and behaviors. Done in this manner, you gain a sense of a moral compass that is endemic to you, embedded in the ground of your own substance. A moral compass emerges that is much stronger than any given to us by society. It is woven out of the fibers of connection that knit everything on and in this planet together.

As a state arising naturally out of the process of leaving old habits behind, becoming your own authority feels like you've finally hit on the truth. Arriving at this awareness level is interesting, and people seem to then branch off into different paths that beckon them onward according to the reality, the lived experience, of who they are.

Becoming your own authority does not mean that suddenly you're going to do whatever you want to do. Our "wants" usually derive from our upbringing, education, perceived insufficiencies (like money, love, sex), attempts at conflict resolution, or cultural expectations. Becoming your own authority happens. It just happens. When you can feel everything about your life, and can start following the course of the next-best-place, it becomes obvious to you that you are indeed the only person who can know what that next-best-place is for you and you won't know what it is until you get there. That is what I mean by becoming your own authority.

It is a condition of being. Not an action you take. It is a condition that comes about through quietness. It takes a certain amount of quiet to attend to what-is. By quiet I don't necessarily mean the noise in the environment. I mean the active chatter of conversation – whether it is within your own head or between people. Using words cuts us off from all of the other functions in our system – all the other processes that are full of information. There is a time to talk and a time to notice. Eventually, with enough practice it may be possible to engage in chatter and notice at the same time. But don't expect that of yourself. If it happens that's great, but most of us are really only good at doing one thing at a time.

Once you can feel your way through life, letting the next-best-place arise and lead you on, it often happens that other people suddenly put themselves forward as authorities about this and that – pressing you to do things their way, conform to their ideas about what is good for you. I don't know why this occurs – perhaps they sense a freedom in you that they don't have, and it may frighten them or make them envious. Try to not take any of this personally – they are merely reacting to something they don't know about with whatever they've learned.

This kind of life is one that requires no master, no guru, no dogma, and no theoretical underpinnings. All of those things can shed light on our experiences, but to use them as paths is unnecessary. Every religious practice or dogma, every scientific theory, every cultural value, limits the field of what we can come to know. Interpretation is a tricky business. The very early Taoists were much like our current scientists – learning from nature. They observed, watched everything that happened, and came to know human nature in that way. They could see how change over time occurred. And they could see how people got in the way of a naturally occurring change and made huge problems for themselves and the rest of the living world. Some tried to write about their knowledge of how this kind of change took place, and how humans could reacquaint themselves with this path. It is a difficult thing to put in words however, as it can only be known by the experience of it. Many of their writings have a mysterious flavor to them – partly the artifact of translating from one language to another, from one era to another, and from a lost culture to a modern one - but also just because there really are no words for the experience of following a naturally occurring path of change instead of deciding what to do next.

When I say "following a naturally occurring path" I do not mean that it is a passive life. Once the next-best-thing has become obvious – and "obvious" is the best word I can find to describe the sensation of change becoming clear – then we often must take action, and sometimes a lot of action. Nothing happens for us. "The Universe" does not just do things for us – we are moving, active creatures with facile brains and facile bodies.

This is when our learned knowledge comes in handy. This is when our brains can start figuring things out – how to get the money together for college, how to get the house sold and move, how to get the plane reservations and where to stay, how to set up an experiment and delve into the secrets of a cell, how to wheel and deal and get a bill through Congress, etc. There is a lot to do in the world, and by becoming your own authority you will put your efforts in the service of this naturally occurring course of change. You will not be going against the grain of what is needed next and will be able to participate in change that makes the next-best-place manifest - instead of making things even more difficult for yourself, other people, or the rest of the world.

# 8: Advanced "Standing Around"

## Awareness, attention, concentration and the problem of escalation

Awareness changes to attention when we *confine* our focus to whatever we became aware of. Attention easily changes to concentration, and when that happens we may be getting into trouble. A overly-focused, concentrated attention on some aspect of ourselves, whether an emotion, a thought, or a physical sensation, may very well cause that aspect to escalate itself. To concentrate on emotions can cause them to build to the point of needing to be acted on. An emotion can surface naturally, be expressed, and if attention does not stay on the emotion, it will subside once its message has been delivered (either to the "emoter" or the "emotee").

If attention is placed on the thought process and the thoughts, then they will become more numerous. If you have a line of thinking you are pursuing, this principal works in your favor. If you are trying to empty your thoughts in a meditation practice, this principle will make it very difficult for you to accomplish this goal.

If attention becomes narrowly focused on a recurring felt sensation then those feelings will escalate sooner or later. I believe that they do not escalate when you first start attending to felt-sense because of how atrophied that ability usually is: those of us in the western cultures have been educated to value thinking, and to use emotions to judge whether we are happy or not. Felt-sense is pretty much ignored and attended to only when discomfort arises. We call it pain, even though much that goes into this category is not really painful – just uncomfortable or strange. So, we have to retrain ourselves to be aware of felt-sense, and it takes awhile for that awareness to settle in and become second nature. Once that happens though, we can choose to concentrate on felt-sense, or even various pieces of it like heartbeat, breathing, etc. There are those who even claim to be able to feel their blood moving through vessels.

Attention can easily turn to concentration – a focused and almost hard-feeling, boring-into kind of noticing. I am not entirely sure this kind of concentration is a good thing. I've noticed that once in awhile someone who has focused their attention to the point of concentration ends up with a physical disease process in the system they've been concentrating on. Just like acting out anger tends to make one very good at getting angry and eventually causing injury to someone else, concentrating over and over again (years, I'm talking about) on some small piece of felt-sense might possibly cause something distressing to happen physically. I'm guessing here...it's a question and a curiosity.

If this is indeed the case, is awareness of felt-sense a good thing or not? Yes, I definitely believe that it is. I don't think you can rid yourself of habitual tendencies or follow the path of naturally occurring change without awareness of felt-sense. But there is a line that gets crossed when attention turns to concentration. It's concentration that I'm not sure is a good thing. It isn't easy to notice when concentration begins, when attention narrows and hardens, and keeps staying focused on the same place or pattern day after day and year after year. This is why I've put this study in the "advanced standing around" category.

For instance, when you first get into 'stand around' position and you become aware of a sensation that you've noticed many times before, let a part of your attention notice the quality of your attention itself. If it feels like it has begun to harden then concentration is happening. Sometimes this is accompanied by strain in the eyes, even though they're probably closed, or tensed facial muscles, or a stiffening of the neck. This means you've actually gone into a goal-oriented action – using the power of your attention to focus. Attention is more loose, or open. If you think you are starting to concentrate, let yourself become aware of more than just your body and your felt-sense – let the other sense faculties come into play and notice what you hear, taste, what your skin feels from the environment. See if you notice that you were straining your eyes or stiffening some muscle group. These actions may have been very subtle, but its interesting material to observe and usually just the observation itself is enough to get you out of the concentration mode.

Play with attention – there are many kinds of attention as you will come to find out. First learn to notice felt-sense, track it, and allow the body to do whatever unwinding it needs without intentional interference. Later, expand your attention to what you feel from outside of you. You may notice nothing at first, and indeed, there may be nothing to notice! Don't push it. Just let the possibility arise. Then play with it – attend to the inner environment, then to the outer environment, then to both at once. Keep it moving and see what happens. This will prevent that fixated concentration and it opens up more paths to knowledge of what-is.

## Unwinding Habits

I've noticed that it is also possible to get into unwinding habits. Once your body starts its unwinding movements, you might notice that each time you "stand around" the same unwinding movement happens over and over. This is fine for the most part. Many of us have very old or well-trained movement habits or defenses that will take a lot of unwinding. But…there's also the possibility that you are developing a new habit: that "standing around" mode equates in your brain now with a particular movement.

How do you tell if this is happening? Well, it's subtle, at least to start with. Say you are well into your third month of "standing around" and as soon as you close your eyes your body takes off into a very familiar twist. At this point you need to ask yourself the question: "am I getting into a habit?" Don't try to do anything about it – just ask the question. Then the next time you "stand around" let your awareness be very open. If there is a habit that is coming into being, your brain will fire the instructions before your body starts to do the movement. This is *very* subtle and nearly instantaneous with the movement, so don't try to find it, or give yourself a hard time if you don't notice anything. There may be nothing to notice.

If there is indeed a habit forming, sooner or later you will catch that firing of instructions in the split second before the twisting starts. But remember, don't try to look for the instructions-thought, just ask the question and let your awareness be loose. Notice *whatever* comes up. It will most likely be something entirely different than what I've noticed. We are developing a vocabulary of functions based entirely on experience so there is never a right or wrong to what shows up. Just "interesting."

One thing to remember with this kind of work – it really doesn't have to all get done now. There's plenty of time. Whatever doesn't happen today can happen tomorrow. Or the next day…

## Rigidities

Anything rigid in the body-system is a limiter. Mental rigidities are big limiters. These encompass assumptions, favorite interpretations and personal stories, the tendency to obsess about past events, or plan future events, etc. Physical rigidities are easier to spot though. Are your shoulders up in your ears and you didn't know it? Or does your head stay off the pillow when you lay down? Are your ankles mobile when you walk or do they stay a bit flexed all the time so that you sort of stump around? Those are the sorts of things to notice. *But not fix.*

Its always so tempting to relax a rigidity once you've noticed it, but if you leave it alone, don't try to keep it rigid and don't try to relax it, then something will happen with it. You won't know what until it happens and you notice it.

Mental rigidities are more elusive and subtle – they just show up and start running before you "know" it. Interpretations of whatever body-sense you are feeling – "this is about my neighbor's sexual abuse, this is about my dog dying…"; or comparing awarenesses with the words of a religious writer; or assumptions of any kind about what is going on; or running through plans of what to do next; or complaints about whoever-did-you-wrong; or any myriad of habitual habits of the brain. Again, becoming aware of them is all you need to do. You may also eventually notice how your system is invested in these stories – it will feel a certain sort of joy, or comfort, or excitement when these thought habits surface. Be aware of those seductive sensations as the thought pattern runs itself, and see what happens next.

These accompanying sensations are more important than the thoughts themselves – they are the glue that keeps the habit in place. It's the glue we're after, so see if you can become aware of the feelings accompanying these kinds of rigidities. They will not want to be noticed, and the seductive attraction will be to go back to thinking the thought – that's where the juicy feel of excitement is. Just notice this tendency to be attracted to the thought and don't resist it. That's the way of conflict again. Just notice the quality and feel of the attraction. That's the animal to track. Get to know everything about it that you can, including that juicy feeling it gives you.

**Noticing the Next Best Thing**

Once tissues and mental processes start to unwind and lose their automatic reactivity, something new starts. A new behavior, noticing something in the environment that you never paid much attention to or wasn't there before...something like that. Its tricky noticing this as the new thing is often very subtle, brief, and easy to miss. This is like a small buried seed that has suddenly put up a little green shoot – easy to miss with all the other greenery around. Don't worry about whether this new thing has surfaced yet – that'll set up an expectation that something new *should* happen and you'll be "standing around" looking for something new. Which gets you right into goal-oriented-ness again. Just keep it a curiosity, and when you get a glimmer that a new energy is afoot, notice it. But don't push at it or for it.

What may happen is that something in your outer environment may suddenly come to your attention – a book, a person, a movie, a meeting, almost anything – and it has an energetic charge to it for you. You feel inexplicably drawn to investigate. So, investigate! One good book opens the next. The initial investigation may not be the pot of gold, but it may very well lead to another path. Or it may turn out that the act of investigating new things is the opening door – not so much the things getting investigated. Remember, the Next Best Thing is a moving target – always opening up in front of you with stops along the way. The naturally occurring path of change never stagnates – there is no perfect place to get to.

There is a painting by Leonardo da Vinci, The Annunciation, that I saw at the Uffizi Gallery in Florence once. It's a stunning thing to stand in front of. Unlike other annunciations where Mary is shown as a shy and reticent young woman, da Vinci's Mary is a purposeful woman in the midst of daily life, reading her book, interrupted suddenly by the appearance of an angel in her garden. She's startled, as any of us would be, but not shy – she actually holds up her hand to catch the words of the angel, accepting this next-best-thing. And this is shown as a mere pause in her reading. This painting is a lovely allegory of what it is like to notice this new thing as it just-now comes into existence. The new shoot is the coming child, the angel is the sudden notification that this has happened, Mary's upraised hand is that so very important awareness of that notification.

This painting is a snapshot of a moment in time that happens for all of us, time and time again. The beginning of the new thing (behavior, unwinding, new meaning, action, circumstance, book, dream, person) must be noticed, and then fixed in our systems by an active awareness of the change that has just taken place. The new-thing is often a very small shift, a subtle change, and it does help to remember that it has indeed happened, and to notice everywhere in our lives that it makes a difference for us. We may feel a little more awareness of beauty when we see the tree outside the window; or notice that we're suddenly tired of making the same kind of verbal response or habitual behavior; or decide the car absolutely must go in for a tune-up soon...notice this small change in awareness. Or we may feel a little less reactive when a chronic pain arises again – notice this lack of reactivity. Noticing the change is important – pushing it, or trying to interpret it is not necessary. There is no need to make it larger than it is. Just noticing what is different is enough. The new-thing, like an embryo, will grow of its own accord. Unlike an embryo, it is our noticing that feeds it, gives it the energy to grow on. But directing it, giving it a story or a numinous meaning, will cause it to mutate, and we will be off the path of naturally occurring change.

This painting also illustrates the helpfulness of having something material, like the lilies the angel is handing off, to remind us every day that this subtle change did indeed occur. It will easily get lost in the habits and stresses of daily life. But if you find a picture or an object to leave in a noticeable place then it becomes a reminder, and that can be helpful as this process unfolds.

Unlike Mary, an angel isn't going to land in our gardens flourishing a bouquet of lilies– wouldn't it be nice if change came with such a trumpeting! But all change, however minor it seems to us at first, is just as big a deal as da Vinci's Annunciation. It might help to think of all our little changes as every bit as important as this big day was for Mary, and that they are all heralded in with a grand flourish, if only we could see it. As we become more aware of the experience of living, these flourishes will become unmistakable and once in awhile, grand indeed.

## The Next-Best-Place Points the Way

Bringing our awareness to the what-is is all we need to do for most of life. But once in awhile (periodically for some of us) we need to do more than that. Sometimes we need to take action, seek medical help, get a new education or a different job. It has been my experience that the tribulations of life often have a pattern to them (this is leaving out the sudden accidents and traumas – the big bangs). Say it's a health problem for simplicity: it starts as a few twinges of something not feeling right; you wait awhile – if it's an illness it'll get bad and go away, if its something else, it'll just get bad; but mostly it stays in the background as an added question-mark during daily life; and then you realize that it not only hasn't gone away, but it's worse and is now getting in the way of daily life; the next realization is that something's got to be done about it – but what?

Most of the time we start doing everything we have already learned that might help, or learning more from whatever sources we can get ahold of, trying this advice and following up on that piece of information. Sometimes you stumble into a route that gets you out of the problem, but often we just keep turning over stones until we get worn out and reach a dead end. At this point we're open to suggestion, and here we can watch ourselves as we get suggestions – because we always do. It might even be necessary to go through the whole process of trying out everything you know or can learn to do before giving up and waiting for suggestion. After all, our ability to learn new things and learn from the past is also a very important adaptation function. We just don't want to get mired in our learned knowledge, become arrogant about what we know, or too sure of ourselves. Those are the Three Horses of the Apocalypse as far as adaptability goes.

The mechanism for how we get matched up with the appropriate therapy, job, house, school, person, or whatever-it-is, is one of our unsolved mysteries. Plenty of people who've experienced this have tried to name it, from god-has-a-plan-for-you to Carl Jung's theory of synergy. The mechanism behind what is essentially a system of connectedness is still an unsolved mystery. In some way, these systems of ours, and evidently everything else in the universe, have an information transfer function – information about ourselves gets out into the world and we get information back. *How* this happens is not going to get solved by me (although I have my own ideas about it, of course!), but it is the experience of this happening that all of us can begin to notice. From the awareness of a "match-up" we can then go on to reap the benefits. We are not out of contact with everyone and everything else going on in the world.

Be careful with this, however. We have another function in our systems that applies meaning to experiences, and we love this function! Humans have been attaching meaning to events, objects, words, and stars for unknown millennia. Figuring out when you're habitually attaching meaning to a surfacing suggestion, and when that suggestion really is one that will lead you in the next-best-direction is a process that's very difficult to put words to - partly because words themselves are meaning-carriers and just the act of reading about how to recognize the "real" suggestion puts a bias into our interpretation function. All I can really do is point out the pitfalls and you will need to flounder around with this one on your own. Well, I can do a bit more than that. I'll try to describe what this process feels like for me.

Back to the bad-health example: when my system needs help from someone else, the route to finding that help becomes obvious via this connection function. The first step is the awareness that I need help - that this problem is beyond my capacity to self-heal. I first turn my attention to noticing everything about what's ailing me – what all of it feels like in detail. Sometimes a thought appears suddenly that illuminates the situation a bit: the history of what happened, something someone else said years ago about this kind of thing, a person to seek advice from. I file that bit of information away and keep it in current time awareness. Sometimes the next route of action is really obvious. It comes with a feeling of definiteness about it. That's a suggestion I take action on. Sometimes it isn't that clear and I can't tell if I'm looking too hard for answers and just making them up. When that happens I wait awhile and see if other suggestions come along. If I really do need help, eventually someone or something will come to my attention with that feeling of certitude to it. There is a sense of "that's it, I'll go see them", instead of something like, "maybe I should check them out" or some other fairly unenthusiastic response. The next-best-therapy feels to me like the other shoe has just dropped and all I have to do is figure out how to get to that person, pay for the therapy, or do whatever is necessary.

Keep in mind that the-next-best-therapy is only what's best right now. We usually need to move on to something or someone else down the road.


**Standing Around with Full Sensory Input**
Once you're comfortably able to access your felt-sense and have become familiar with the unwinding process you can bring the world back into play as well. "Stand around" with your eyes open, using all of your senses to add to the conscious information load you are already taking in through internal felt-sense and thought-awareness. I think it's easier to tackle this by first going for walks outdoors, and each time out focus on what you are aware of through one sense only. Start with eyes and notice every little detail of a bush or a bird as you walk by it. Then do the same with hearing, smelling, kinesthetic (the air on your face, the feel of the ground) and lastly, taste. Taste may seem like an odd one to use on a walk, but our taste receptors bring a lot of information to us about the environment. Let your jaw be slightly slack at first and you will begin to notice slight flavors in the air. Then practice being aware of the sensory input from all senses at once.

Once you've made friends with walking in the world aware of all sensory feedback, find a place to sit or stand and bring your attention to the whole panoply of sensation coming at you through your externally oriented sensory receptors, your internal felt sense, and "thought-watcher"/"emotion-detector". It's a lot to track at once, and one of the benefits of it is that you are so busy tracking everything that there is no focus left for getting caught on habits. You will be entirely in present-time and can choose which habitual actions to take or not to take. Sometimes we even get a chance to glimpse matter and energy without the limitations of what we've learned to expect.

Once you've trained your system to do non-intentional attention and unwound enough habitual thought and behavior patterns so that this kind of attention has become second nature, retrain yourself during daily life to bring non-intentional attention into play more often. An easy place to begin to do this is during a heated argument. These are very stressful for us, so easy events to notice, unlike most of the routines of daily life.

# 9: Extras

## Boundaries

A new "should-be", especially for those in the non-allopathic healing professions, is the injunction to have good boundaries. "We *must* have boundaries between our clients and ourselves".

Must we? Or might this have become another energy-exhausting expectation?

Let's explore this a bit. A boundary is something that creates a "me" and "not-me". It is first about identity. As we've seen earlier, to identify your self as this or that is to keep yourself locked into habitual programming. You become less adaptable. Variability escapes you. Boundaries are structures (whether material or energetic) that create separateness, conflict and eventually warfare.

On the other end of the spectrum we have osmosis. A process of mixing - differently identifiable things filter into each other's space until there is an even spacing. It's a slow travelling back and forth through a medium. It is not a take-over and squelch invasion – not an attempt to overrun space, but to share it.

So many relationships turn into a fight as the parties try to change each other to suit themselves better. The sense of sharing life is overwhelmed by the sense of controlling it. A boundary is the first step in setting up control-over. If that's you on that side, and me on this side, then we know as soon as someone transgresses. An injustice has just happened, and self-righteousness gets to have a field day. And don't we all get a kick out of feeling self-righteous?

A boundary locks people into an identity that will come to need defending. A different idea to try on is that there is no boundary between people – we might have skin covering us and showing where I stop and you begin, but what about thoughts, emotions, energy? They don't stop at the skin. What actually happens if you let someone else's state of being enter and mix with yours? If you are aware of it, paying attention, you'll get to notice how you change, what new information is now available, perhaps things happen that you didn't know were possible.

We have this idea that someone else's energy will only harm us, or control us, or suck our energy out of us. And yes, that does happen when we are all running on un-observed neural programming. That's the control-over habit. But if you are watching the whole interaction with acute awareness, without monkeying around with it at all, the other person will have just had their manipulative option stymied. Even in the presence of someone very consciously trying to invade your emotional space, that invasion will turn into something else when it does not meet with the expected resistance. When it is met with an acute observation of its actions, something else will happen. It's an interesting experience – give it try some time.


## Metaphors

A good metaphor can be very helpful with some of this non-logical work. They can be helpful reminders during daily life. One of Marvin Solit's favorite metaphors for this work was to think of the body as a factory of workers and the mind as the manager. The manager gives orders, and the workers do what they're told. The workers might have noticed a better way to do their work, or that something was not functioning well, but with the manager/worker setup that information had no route upwards. Orders went downwards, nothing went upwards. So with the "standing around" we're giving the workers (the rest of the non-brain body) a chance to strut their stuff, have input, lead for a bit while management follows for a change. It is a time for the workers to let information flow upwards and for the management to listen and not direct. This simplifies what's going on and makes it an easy abstraction to hang on to.

Another metaphor the early community used was the immune system/repair system dichotomy. The immune system is all about identifying "me" vs. "them", going into attack mode to take out the intruders and hauling off the corpses. The repair system was about letting the body find its own mechanism to repair damage. We know, of course, that the repair function is really the second part of the immune response in humans. Identify and kill the invaders, then repair the damage. One follows the other. So it's not a perfect metaphor, but the idea was to consider how we use the Overseer part of our conscious mind as the thing that always searches for the problems and then for the fixes. It's what has become the symptomatic approach in allopathic medicine as well as many alternative health care professions. With this metaphor you have an easy handle to remind yourself to watch how many times you look for a "problem" and then for a "fix" and then go after the problem with the fix – attack mode in other words. We're always attacking problems. When you first start "standing around" this will happen often – something starts becoming painful or at least noticeable in a negative way and the first impulse is to figure out what's wrong, give it meaning, then find a solution. When this happens just say to yourself – "oh, I'm in attack mode again, let me just put that to the side for now". Go back to plain observation and see what happens next.

# 10: The Movement of Thoughts

The first step was to bring the body back into our awareness and to learn to take it seriously again. Hopefully by now, the whole idea of a body and mind that are two distinct entities will seem absurd. Emotions, thoughts, sensations and feelings have become fragmented only because that is our perception of them.

Thoughts have movement, just like bodies. Between one thought and another is a fragment of time, one thought moving on, unfolding into the next. Hopefully you've been able to experience yourself creating movement habits – the motor cortex launching a new piece of software that it's developed because something got repeated more than three times. This is an automatic function that our brains may be programmed to do, but even so, a repeated movement can still be prevented from becoming a habit if our attention is very acute.

Similarly, thoughts become habitual as well. These are more subtle for us and perhaps more charged emotionally. After all, most of us identify with our thoughts – the thinker is "me", and "me" is in control and decides what's what. The idea that some of these wonderful thoughts are mere habitual outpourings is a bit disconcerting. But it's worse than that. If you have become very observant of your felt sense, and been able to track it through many different experiences, you may have had the experience by now of observing a thought arise followed by a particular felt sense experience. The thought seems to be a verbal print out of whatever issue the body is having that results in the physical symptom that follows shortly after the thought. The thought may not have been very accurate, but it was the best the brain could do to approximate what the body was experiencing. Remember, our brains are entirely educated – if there is not a word in its learned vocabulary that matches what is going on in the whole system, or there is no word with a meaning that directly matches, then the brain has to choose words that are pretty close. Or maybe it chooses a past experience, or book, or movie, whose meaning to you approximates what is happening currently. These kinds of thoughts I call "The Verbal Printout". They are not creative, they are not figured out, they are put together by the brain without any volition on the part of the "thinker".

Another non-volitional thought is the Associative Thought. Our brains keep track of similarities between things and sends input into categories based on those similarities. When new input gets categorized with other similar content, our brains send us a thought about those similarities and we perceive it as having just made an intriguing association between things. We are often greatly excited by these kinds of thoughts, thinking that we've just found connections between two seemingly unrelated things or people or events. So then we set about attributing meaning to these similarities that our brain has called our attention to. (Starfish have 5 appendages, so do humans, and we draw stars with 5 points…therefore the number 5 has a cosmic importance of mystical significance, etc.) This association however was most likely not "figured out", but merely the result of synapses firing in the presence of similarities and waving a metaphorical flag to get our attention. It's a "look at this" notification, not a major creative act. It is then necessary to observe the associative thought and decide whether the similarities it is showing us have meaning or not. They may very well not be important at all.

The point I'm trying to make is that many of our thoughts are the result of the brain just doing what it does. The lungs breathe and we don't think much about it. But the brain spits out thoughts and we think there is a "me" creating all these thoughts. But it may not be so – there may be many thoughts that are the result of information links and synapse firing that is as rote as the lungs breathing oxygen in and $CO_2$ out. Other thoughts then come into question. We have all been annoyed by obsessive thoughts. Or tried to change our thinking about something and found that it is a lot of effort. How much of our thinking is truly volitional? How much of it ought to be? We can create a habit of how we attend to our thoughts. If we think these Associative Thoughts or Verbal Printouts have been created by the thinker and thus have great importance, we will always attend to them as if they had great importance. This perception will nail in the habit of giving great credence to all thoughts. So there becomes a *perception* of thoughts that can be habitual, just like the thoughts themselves can be habitual. Sort of an "uber-thought" about thoughts. (!)

For instance: a person has a habit of watching television every evening. They also have brought with them from childhood an admonishment that watching television is not something an intelligent person should do. So the thought arises after dinner, "I think I'll go turn on the TV" and concurrently the next thought arises "I shouldn't be watching TV, it's only for stupid people". And they go ahead and watch TV, with the second thought running in the background. Both thoughts are habits of long standing. The second thought is a perception of the first one, and is actually the thought that is creating conflict in that person's system with whatever resulting havoc that might be wreaked.

These secondary thoughts – the perceptions about a thought that's just occurred – are very important for us to observe. There is much habit embedded in thoughts like this. These secondary thoughts can actually repeat themselves endlessly. But they can be observed as well, just like we observe felt sense:
Without evaluation, any sense of what we'd rather be thinking, just an attitude of discovery, of wanting to observe the entirety of this habit, and see what happens next once its been observed.

My experience with observing these "uber-thoughts" is that once they've been observed in this manner they fall apart suddenly. It's like trying to catch air – they were there, and now they're not. It seems that if they can be truly observed in this fashion they do not return as habitual thoughts. In fact, perception feels cleaner, as if you've just washed the lenses of your glasses. They do return as memories, and offer themselves as options for how to think about the current thought. But as memories they are no longer on automatic, no longer a conditioned, habitual reaction to a particular kind of thought. As a memory we are no longer under their control.

But, don't let my experience with this lead you on. Find and observe your "uber-thoughts", your secondary thoughts. See what happens. You will need to have brought great energy to your observation in order to see the entirety of these kinds of thoughts. But it's a very interesting experience – fun even! Remember, I am not a teacher for you in this. I am just someone who would like to bring it to your attention that other possibilities exist for how we can live. This way of living has no technique, no methodology, no predictable outcome. It is life as a constantly creative act by acute self-observation. It is a way to use consciousness to guide ourselves out of what has taken the place of instinct – habit. Conditioning. Education. Culture. Socialization. All of these create a human that runs on habit – half aware, half here, pretty much on automatic pilot. Self reflection is our way out of this automaton state.

# 11: Some Final Cheerleading

I realize that much of what I've written about non-intentional awareness sounds very challenging to actually accomplish, and there is something difficult about it that I haven't ever been able to clearly understand. Perhaps it's some self-preservation brain function that doesn't want to be looked at too closely because things will indeed change. But that is really the only challenging part.

Reading about this process is more challenging than just doing it. It can help a lot to become acquainted with the process through the aid and presence of others. Not someone to point the direction, just someone to help you notice when you're being intentional as that seems to be the truly invisible elephant in the room at first. An "exogenous observer" can help you get to the point where you can notice your directedness. Once you can see that, you're on your way.

It may sound narcissistic to be so self-observational, but in fact, it is just the opposite. Most of our habitual conditioned reactions and responses in this world are the result of self-preservation. Habits get so dug in that it becomes self-preservation way beyond any real necessity. Self-observation reduces the reign of habit in our systems and momentarily stalls-out the control of the conditioned response. We are more able to see situations clearly, without reference to us, and to respond more appropriately to what is happening exactly now instead of being driven by experiences from the past, the should-be's of our culture or upbringing, the education of the era.

Adaptability is limited with learned responses. With consciousness, humans have taken the next step away from being totally run by our brains to being able to short-circuit the automaton in our heads at least long enough to see it running. This is actually a huge step in evolution. Being able to create a self-monitoring feedback loop that can notice conditioned responses, is a major event. We certainly can't intervene in all of them, nor would we want to, but many of these responses are not always the best ones for the circumstance at hand. Only when we can see our habits do we have a chance to move past their limitations.

This opportunity called consciousness is an opportunity not to be missed. So far we have used it sloppily, taken it for granted, used it to willpower our way past our limitations, tried reductionist experimentation on it, but we have not done much conscious exploration with it experientially. "Standing around" is one way to explore and at the same time, one way to change our lives in many different ways – physically, behaviorally, emotionally, and above all, unexpectedly.

# 12: Further Information

For a thorough, highly readable update on the current neuroscience about brain function that will show you what we're up against with the automaton in our heads see:
Eagleman, David, *Incognito*, Pantheon Books; NY, 2011.

www.fnd.org is a website for The Foundation for New Directions. This is the organization set up by Marvin Solit and a community of early explorers into this phenomenon of non-directed, non-intentional movements. The early impetus was around health care, but explorations soon led into many different fields. See this website for articles and to contact some of Dr. Solit's fellow explorers.

To email Marilyn Beech with questions or requests for workshops: marilynbeech@gmail.com.

Made in the USA
Charleston, SC
27 June 2016